W9-CRO-809

Grandma, Aren't You Glad the World's Finally in Color Today!

By Lori Stewart

Palmar Press - California

Published by Palmar Press, Carmel, CA
Printed in the United States of America

First Edition, 2014

Publisher's Cataloging-In-Publication Data
(Prepared by The Donohue Group, Inc.)

Stewart, Lori.
  Grandma, aren't you glad the world's finally in color today! / by Lori Stewart. -- First edition.

  pages : illustrations (some color) ; cm

  Summary: A story in rhyme that takes readers on a "then and now" journey through time as a grandmother compares her mother's life and times to those of her grandchildren. This is a conversation-starter book that encourages readers to share their own family history.
  ISBN: 978-0-9839293-1-4 (hardcover)

  1. Grandmothers--Family relationships--Juvenile literature. 2. United States--Social life and customs--20th century--Juvenile literature. 3. United States--History--20th century--Juvenile literature. 4. Grandparent and child--Juvenile literature. 5. Families--History--Juvenile literature. 6. Grandmothers--Family relationships. 7. United States--Social life and customs--20th century. 8. United States--History--20th century. 9. Grandparent and child. 10. Families--History. 11. Stories in rhyme. I. Title.

E161 .S749 2014
973.9

www.palmarpress.com

To the greatest generations, and those to come!

Lou Stewart

School's out for summer, we're off to the shore,
To Grandmother's cottage, a place we love more
Than theme parks or road trips or astronaut camps,
For a ding-hummer summer with Grandma and Gramps!

Our grandmother's house is a very old place.
It squeaks when you walk or just stand in one space.
The rooms are quite cozy and full of fun things,
Like dishes of candy and old diamond rings;
Rocking chairs, tchotchkes in crannies and nooks;
Vases of flowers and walls of old books.
Way up at the top, the books that most mattered
Are faded and dusty, all timeworn and tattered.

"I wonder what those are?" we say to ourselves,

As we climb on each other to reach the high shelves.

We snatch the old books from the place where they lay,

And then out of nowhere we hear Grandma say,

"Those are the family albums, my dears,

Full of old photos of life through the years.

They tell us the story of our family tree,

From the time of my mother and father to me.

Let's thumb through these pages," our grandmother said,

"While I tell you stories I've stored in my head!"

1902		1920		1926		1928
Carrier invented the air conditioner in 1902. Home air conditioning came in the 1920s, enabling the great migration to the Sun Belt.	Special Relativity Theory proposed by Einstein in 1905 becomes widely accepted in the physics community by the 1920s. **1905**	My mother, your mother's grandmother, your great-grandmother is born.	*Time*, the first weekly news magazine in the US is founded by Briton Hadden and Henry Luce. **1923**	The Model T came in colors in 1916 until Ford said customers could order a Model T in any color as long as it was black. Ford made red Model Ts again in 1926!	First talking movie is *The Jazz Singer*. The Golden Age of Jazz continues from 1920-1933. **1927**	Penicillin is discovered by Scottish scientist Alexander Fleming.

"It all started way back, way back in the day,

When cameras were Brownies and photos were grey;

Back in the time before daylight was saved;

Before atoms were split, or the highways were paved;

Before penicillin injections were shot;

Before Relativity Theory got hot;

				Daylight savings time was enacted by FDR during WWII. Congress adopted it in 1918 but repealed it in 1919.	
The first ice-cube tray patent is granted to Guy Tinkham.	*1933*	*Life*, the first photo magazine in the U.S., cost a dime in 1936.	*1937*		*1946*	
1933	FDR takes the U.S. off the gold standard.	*1936*	The paving of Route 66, "The Main Street of America" is completed, linking Chicago, IL to Santa Monica, CA.	*1942*	The first Electronic Numeric Integrator and Computer (ENIAC) is built for the U.S. Army at the University of Pennsylvania.	

Before the computer was ever envisioned;

And way long before all the air was conditioned;

Long before ice cubes or red Model Ts;

Before movies could talk, before jazz and TVs;

When gold was the standard and LIFE cost a dime;

In fact, it was just a few years before TIME,"

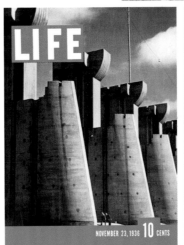

4

First four-way, three-color traffic light is created by a police officer, William Potts, in Detroit, MI.

1921

1920

The Band-Aid is invented by Earle Dickson.

The Golden Gate Bridge opens, linking San Francisco with Marin County.

1940

1937

Stone Age cave paintings are discovered in Lascaux, France by four kids looking for their dog.

First Jeep is invented - possibly named after Eugene the Jeep, Popeye's magical "jungle pet" who could solve all problems!

1941

1961

The Peace Corps is established by President Kennedy.

"That here in this room, on one bright summer's morn,

Your great-grandmother - MY mother - was born!

She had straight brown hair, big green eyes and two feet,

Upon which she'd hop, skip and jump up the street,

Then '*race off to school, twenty miles on most days,*

Barefoot, through snowdrifts and uphill both ways'!

On special occasions, she might take the trolley,

Or trot with a friend on a pony, by golly!

| Ronald Reagan is elected President of the United States. | **1981** | The Channel Tunnel, "The Chunnel" opens, connecting Britain and France. | **1999** | The Segway PT self-balancing personal transport is unveiled. | **2009** |
| **1980** | NASA's first space shuttle, Columbia, rockets into orbit. | **1994** | First razor scooter is distributed by Sharper Image. | **2001** | Water is discovered on the moon. |

You kids ride to school in a big yellow bus,

Or a family van that is chauffeured by us!

You might ride your bikes on a bright sunny day,

Or skateboard to school if it's not far away."

Big Bang Theory is first proposed by George LaMaitre, a Belgian physicist and priest.	*1929*	The Dust Bowl causes severe drought, forcing mid-west farmers to migrate to the west.	*1935*	Grand Rapids, MI is the first city to fluoridate its water.	*1944*		
1927	Richard Byrd makes the first flight to the Antarctic.	*1933*	Hoover Dam, which spans the Colorado River, is completed.	*1941*	Ball point pens go on sale.		

"Great-Grandma's old school house had only one room;

A blackboard with chalk, and some desks and a broom;

A potbellied stove that would keep the place hot,

While 'ithmatic, reading and writing were taught!

7

Today your fine school seems to have several wings

For art, math and music; a playground with swings;

An organic garden; a field for each sport;

A theater stage; an official mock court;

Labs and libraries all totally wired;

Powered by solar and eco-inspired!"

| Kellogg sells the first corn flakes. | *1924* | Sliced bread is invented in Davenport, Iowa by Otto Rohwedder. | *1930* | Sunflower oil is first used to make margarine. | *1954* |
| *1906* | Clarence Birdseye develops frozen foods. | *1928* | Chocolate chip cookies are invented by Ruth Wakefield at her Toll House Inn, MA. | *1944* | Dr. Salk begins to inoculate children against polio. |

"Back then after school children used to do chores,
Like hanging out laundry and sweeping up floors;
Feeding the chickens and peeling potatoes;
Canning ripe strawberries, yams and tomatoes.

| Dead Sea Scrolls are discovered 1947-1956. | **1963** | Title IX legislation is signed, and has a far reaching impact on women in sports. | **1989** | Hubble telescope is carried into orbit by the Space Shuttle. | **2001** |
| **1956** | Alcatraz, San Francisco's island penitentiary, is closed. | **1972** | Berlin Wall is torn down, opening East Germany to the West after 28 years. | **1990** | Wikipedia is launched by Jimmy Wales and Larry Sanger, using the concept and technology of a *wiki*. |

Today after school, kids are doing … who knows?

Practicing music and dancing on toes;

Riding and boating and fishing with Gramps;

Invention conventions and leadership camps."

10

		Zippers replace hook and eye closures and beat out the button in the "battle of the fly!"		Peanut cartoon strip first appears as *L'il Folks*, and becomes *Peanuts* in 1950.	
Pink bubble gum is invented by Walter Diemer.	*1935*		*1937*		*1950*
1928	Nylon is invented, and used to replace silk in stockings.	*1935*	The T-Shirt becomes popular as a slip on garment without buttons.	*1947*	Birth of ready-to-wear clothing standardizes sizing for the fashion industry.

"Back then girls wore pinafore dresses to school;
Middies and sweaters of good Shetland wool;
Mary Jane shoes with bright white cotton socks;
Bloomers for play peeked out under their frocks!
The boys all wore corduroy pants or short knickers,
And sailor suits under their yellow rain slickers;
Argyle socks and un-buckled galoshes,
For jumping in puddles and splashing through swashes.

Bikini is introduced by Louis Réard, a French mechanical engineer, and Jacques Heim.	**1950**		Mary Quant introduces the first miniskirt, and names it after the Mini Cooper - her favorite car.	**2007**		The Royal Wedding of Prince William and Kate Middleton takes place in London.	**2013**
1946	First credit card is conceived by Frank McNamara after a "Diners Club" dinner.		**1964**	Saggy pants are banned in Atlanta schools.		**2012**	Diffus creates the *Climate Dress* with LEDs that detect pollution.

Today all you kids lounge around with ebooks,

Sporting your colorful high fashion looks:

Orange and blue tights, ruffled skirts and pink shrugs;

Bubble puff jackets and bright purple Uggs;

T-shirts with graphics; red board shorts to swim in;

Sun-faded jeans in bright neon persimmon;

Fleece sherpa hoodies with zippers and plackets;

Sequins and gem flowers pinned on your jackets."

12

Teddy Bear is introduced, and named after Teddy Roosevelt, who refused to shoot a bear.	*1916*	Monopoly game is first sold by Parker Brothers.	*1944*	Slinky Toy hits the shelves in New York.	*1958*
1902	Miniature golf is first introduced in Pinehurst, NC.	*1934*	Silly Putty is invented by accident during research for a potential rubber substitute.	*1945*	Legos bricks are introduced in their present form. Lego comes from "leg godt," Danish for "play well."

"Back then the Depression made everyone poor,

So Great-Grandma learned to turn less into more.

She sewed some new dresses from old flour bags;

Curled hair into ringlets with long cotton rags.

She found that the best things in life were all free;

Laughter, long friendships, a sweet melody;

Good graces, God's blessings, a bit of good luck;

The wisdom of ages, raw courage and pluck!

When friends came around, they were quite contented

To play the board games that had JUST been invented:

Scrabble and Sorry, Monopoly too,

With shiny bright tokens like iron and shoe.

Today all you children have many more toys:

Ribbon sticks, slack lines, crayons that make noise;

Leapsters and soakers, and green submarines;

And Goldie Blox boxes with Spinning Machines;

Butterfly Gardens and Sing-A-Ma-Jigs;

Robotic black bugs, and pink pillow pet pigs;

Flutter-by fairies and kits to make gums;

Magnetic brain puzzles, and tubas and drums!"

14

First Academy Awards ceremony takes place at a private dinner in Los Angeles.

1938

Color TV is introduced. *Tournament of Roses Parade* is the first national color broadcast.

1957

The Sound of Music opens on Broadway.

1969

1929

Snow White and the Seven Dwarfs is the first full-length animated cartoon. Superman appears in comic books.

1952

Dr. Seuss's *The Cat in the Hat* is published.

1959

Sesame Street first airs and becomes the longest running American childrens' television series.

"Back then television was as yet unknown,

So kids went to town to where movies were shown:

A grand Picture Palace with red velvet seats;

A Wurlitzer organ and free ice cream treats!

They'd listen to records; read books old and new -

The Wizard of Oz and old *Winnie the Pooh*.

At night, every family across the whole nation

Tuned into their favorite radio station.

They'd listen to Roosevelt's fireside chat;

Jack Benny, The Shadow and Felix the Cat.

They'd call up their friends from the old closet hall,

Where a telephone hung on a hook on the wall!

15

Today kids watch programs, play games and send notes

Through screens on computers, TVs with remotes;

Laptops and tablets, smartphones for the masses;

Game boys and players, iWatches, and glasses!

You email and text friends, and call and then tweet them;

Then hangout on Facebook and hope you can meet them!

And just when we think that your track is all wrong,

You shoot a great movie, compose a hot song;

Create a few widgets, from bytes, bits and bobs;

Then start a new venture, and give us all jobs!"

16

		Babe Ruth hits his 714th home run, a record that would stand for nearly 40 years.		Disneyland opens its first theme park in Anaheim, CA.	
The first Olympic Winter Games are held in Chamonix, France.	*1926*		*1953*		*1958*
1924	Gertrude Ederle becomes the first woman to swim the English Channel.	*1935*	Sir Edmund Hillary and Tenzing Norgay climb Mt. Everest, the highest mountain on earth (from sea level).	*1955*	Hula Hoop is invented by Arthur K. Melin and Richard Knerr.

"Back then the old sandlot was where kids would meet,

Or they would play stickball right there in the street;

Jump rope and shoot marbles, play tag in the park;

Or hide and go seeking until it got dark.

Today your play spaces amaze and astound us,

Bursting with color and sound all around us:

A dodecahedron; a full skateboard park;

With cradles and tunnels that glow in the dark;

A bright colored forest of hand-knitted rings;

A mobius strip, and rotating rope swings!

You master new skills as you follow the path,

Like climbing and timing, and balance and math!"

18

| Charleston dance becomes the rage. | **1935** | First gold record is given to Glenn Miller for his million selling hit, *Chattanooga Choo Choo.* | **1946** | Bebop emerges as the new dance craze. | **1954** |
| **1920** | Shirley Temple receives a special Juvenile Academy Award for *Curley Top.* | **1942** | Frank Sinatra releases first album, *The Voice of Frank Sinatra.* | **1949** | Elvis Presley first appears on *The Ed Sullivan Show.* |

"Back then kids would dance to the sound of big bands,
And jitterbug, jive, lindy-hop holding hands.
Jazz, blues and sweet music, the 'Era of Swing',
When Ellington, Basie and Goodman were king;
When young Shirley Temple excelled at her arts,
And tap danced straight into America's hearts!

The Beatles tour the U.S., launching popular music's British invasion.	*1965*	The first Woodstock Music and Art Fair - three days of peace and music - is held at Max Yasgur's dairy farm.	*1977*	Michael Jackson, "The King of Pop," releases *Thriller*, the most influential pop music video of all time.	*2005*
1964	Rolling Stones release mega hit song, *(I can't get no) Satisfaction*.	*1969*	*Saturday Night Fever* popularizes disco music.	*1982*	YouTube is launched by Chad Hurley, Steve Chen, and Jawed Karim, former PayPal employees.

Today there are so many styles of dance -

Hip Hop and New Wave, Electro and Trance.

You kids dance in circles and swirl your scarves;

Do Dougie and Runningman dances with stars;

Snap fingers and toes, touch your shoulders and knees;

'Whip your hair back and forth'; 'trip the light' if you please!"

20

The stock market crashes, triggering the Great Depression.	1931	The Loch Ness Monster is first spotted by Alex Campbell, the water bailiff for Loch Ness.	1936	Mount Rushmore, the "Presidents' Mountain", is completed in the Black Hills of South Dakota.	1945
1929	The Empire State Building, designed by William Lamb, is completed.	1933	Social Security is enacted in U.S.	1941	United Nations is founded to stop wars between countries, and to provide a platform for dialogue.

"Back then the Depression dragged on more and more,

And then on its heels came the second big war.

Young men were all drafted and shipped out to sea

To watch o'er the ramparts and keep us all free.

Great Grandma was eager to help with all that,

So she took off her gloves, and put on a new hat.

She rolled up her sleeves, and worked several years,

Designing new airplanes and switches and gears.

21

Right after V-Day, at the end of the War,

A handsome young soldier moved in right next door!

Great-Grandma smiled and flashed her green eyes,

And for that lucky lad, music filled up the skies.

It was love at first sight for the rest of her life,

So they both pledged their troth and became man and wife!

They floated along, happily as could be,

And then had my sisters and brothers and me!"

| The Polaroid camera is invented. | **1947** | Your grandmother is born. | **1959** | Secretariat, an American Thoroughbred racehorse, wins the Triple Crown. | **1990** |
| **1947** | Unidentified flying object is reported landing in Roswell, NM. | **1949** | Alaska and Hawaii are the last two states admitted to the union. | **1974** | Adobe Photoshop is invented. |

"The End!" Grandma said, as she closed the first book,
And gave the old album one fond final look.
"Now off you go, go on outside and play,
While I straighten up and put these things away."

23

We all ran outside, but then turned right around,

And came running back to the house with a bound.

We all started shouting out, "Grandma come quick!"

And snatched up our smart phones, and started to click

At the glow of the sunset's chromatic display -

A spectrum of colors, not one of them grey!

"Grandma," we exclaimed as it melted away,

"Aren't you glad the world's finally in color today!"

Photo Credits in Order of Appearance

Dedication Page
Family Reunion © Whatthano/Dreamstime

Introduction
Grandma's Cottage, Photograph by Gandzjuk, Private Collection
Old Private Library Shelves © Chris Nolan/Dreamstime
Old Books Shelves © Kseniya Ragoina/Dreamstime
Three Old Photo Albums © Ronalds Stikans/Dreamstime
Family Album © Private Collection

Timeline
Daylight Savings Time © Unkreatives/Dreamstime
Mushroom Cloud with Ships below during Operation Crossroads Nuclear Weapons Test on Bikini Atoll, Repository: Library of Congress Prints and Photographs Division LC-DIG-ds-02945
Route 66 © Joop Kleuskens/Dreamstime
Dr. Alexander Fleming with Petri Dish, Production of Penicillin Collection, Prints and Photographs Division, Library of Congress, LC-US62-92562
Albert Einstein Speaking, Harris & Ewing 1940, Repository, Prints and Photographs Division, Library of Congress, LC-DIG-hec-28667
ENIAC Computer, U.S. Army Photo, from K. Kempf, "Historical Monograph: Electronic Computers within the Ordnance Corps" The ENIAC, in BRL building 328.
Red Model T © Kathryn Sidenstricker/Dreamstime
The Jazz Singer Theatrical Release Poster 1927, Wikimedia Commons
LIFE Magazine Cover 1936 © Photo of Cover, original photo by Margaret-Bourke-White, Life Magazine.
TIME Magazine Cover 1923, Wikimedia Commons

Getting to School – Then
Young Girl in Snowsuit © Private Collection
Horse School Bus Trolley, Courtesy of Western History/Genealogy Department, Denver Public Library.
Children on Pony Riding to School © George Bell/Tyrell Photographic Collection, Registration 85/1284-227.

Getting to School – Today
Yellow School Bus © Chris Nolan/Dreamstime
Kids Riding to School in Van © Randy Faris/Corbis
Riding Bikes to School © Dasharosato/Dreamstime
Kids skateboarding to School © Kevin Dodge/Corbis

School Houses – Then
One Room Schoolhouse, Photograph by Marion Post Wolcott, Prints and Photographs Division, Library of Congress, LC-USF34-055838-D

Schools – Then (continued)
School House Hinkletown, PA, Photograph by John Collier, Prints and Photographs Division, Library of Congress, LC-USF34-082309-D
Hanasupai Indian School, Cataract Canyon, Photograph by Henry Greenwood, Prints and Photographic Division, Library of Congress, LC USZ 62-11672

Schools – Today
Aerial School Campus, San Domenico Photograph
Violinist © Longfield/Private Collection
Horse Jumping © Verville/Private Collection
Lacrosse Practice © Private Collection
Soccer Practice © Peter Mautsch/Maranso Gmbh/Dreamstime
Soccer Girl © Longfield/Private Collection
Three Girls on Slide © ESchlemmer/Private Collection
Boy Sliding down Yellow Tube © PCooper/Private Collection
Boy with Shark Girl © Shortt Private Collection

After School Activities – Then
Removing Laundry from Line, Photograph by Russell Lee, Prints and Photographic Division, Library of Congress LC-USF33-011883-M3
Feeding Chickens, W.E.B. Du Bois, Collector, Prints and Photographic Division, Library of Congress LC-USZ62-124867
Girl Sweeping, Photograph by Marjorie Collins, Prints and Photographic Division, Library of Congress LC-USW3-026224-D
Canning Tomatoes, South Carolina, Photograph by Marion Post Wolcott, Prints and Photographic Division, Library of Congress LC-USF34-051917-D

After School Activities – Today
Practicing Music © Wheeler Private Collection
Dancing on Toes, © Rogers Private Collection.
Mountain Biking © Boitano Private Collection
Inner Tube Boat © Wheeler Private Collection
Riding © Dupree Private Collection
Water Skiing © Private Collection
Fishing with Gramps © Thomas Perkins/Dreamstime
Invention Convention © Tim Pannell/Corbis

School Fashion – Then
Pinafore Dresses © Newcastle Libraries
Bloomers, MaryJanes, Vandegrift/Private Collection
First Graders Washington DC, Prints and Photographic Division, Library of Congress, LC-USZ62-107103
Cabinet Children at White House Easter Egg Roll, Prints and Photographic Division, Library of Congress, LC-USZ62-131887
Unbuckled Galoshes © Milosluz/Dreamstime

Please visit us at www.palmarpress.com to learn more about building your own family tree.